SUNSETS
TO COLOR

THUNDER BAY
P·R·E·S·S

San Diego, California

Thunder Bay Press
An imprint of Printers Row Publishing Group
9717 Pacific Heights Blvd, San Diego, CA 92121
www.thunderbaybooks.com • mail@thunderbaybooks.com

Printers Row Publishing Group is a division of Readerlink Distribution Services, LLC.
Thunder Bay Press is a registered trademark of Readerlink Distribution Services, LLC.

This edition contains illustrations previously published in *52 Sunsets*, © 2019.

Correspondence regarding the content of this book should be sent to Thunder Bay Press, Editorial Department, at the above address.

Publisher: Peter Norton • Associate Publisher: Ana Parker
Art Director: Charles McStravick
Senior Developmental Editor: April Graham
Editor: Julie Chapa
Production Team: Beno Chan, Mimi Oey, Rusty von Dyl

Cover and interior illustrations: Josh Figueroa
Illustrations on pages 16, 20, 21, 35, 36, 37, 40, 49, 52, 57, 58, 59, 60, 61: Vlasenko Katy/Shutterstock.com
Illustrations on page 17: JoyImage/iStock via Getty Images
Illustrations on page 42: Sybirko/iStock via Getty Images

ISBN: 978-1-6672-0147-4

Printed, manufactured, and assembled in Dongguan, China

26 25 24 23 22   1 2 3 4 5

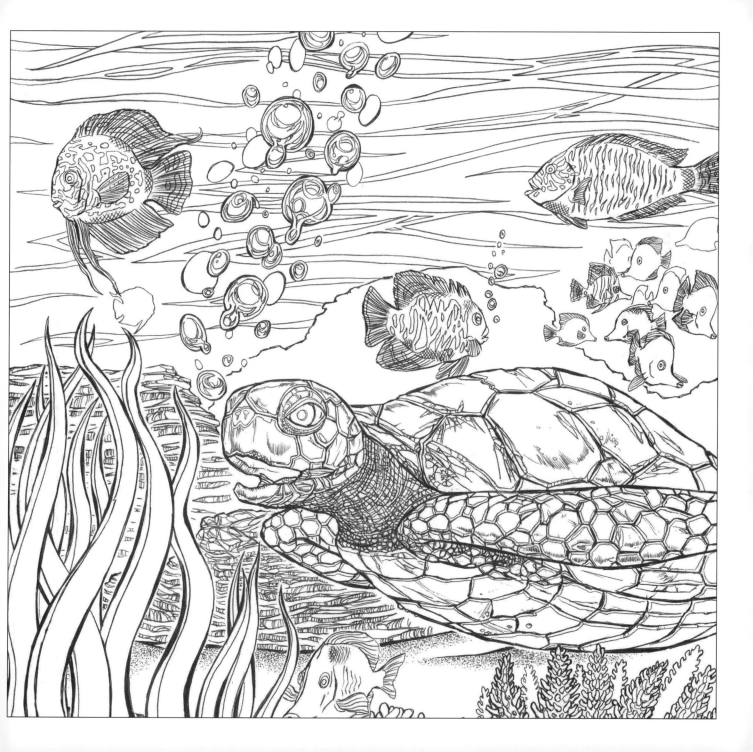